Breathwork Journey Workbook

Ciara Longman

Written and researched by Ciara Longman.

Although the author has taken all reasonable care in preparing this book
at the time of research, no warranty is accepted concerning the accuracy
or completeness of its content.

Facilitated Rebirthing Breathwork sessions with a professionally trained
Rebirther must accompany the use of this workbook. The author
disclaims all liability arising from use of this workbook.

This book is intended only for people taking a series of 10 breathwork sessions. This book is for those who have committed to having sessions with a professionally trained Rebirthing Breathworker.

Check: www.BreathworkAlliance.com or www.RebirthingAssociation.com for Rebirthers certified to professional and ethical standards.
For advice on a choosing a rebirther, read this article: https://breathtalks.com/choosing-rebirther/

This book takes you through each session, provides practical theory and pointers for journalling.
If you are ready to take responsibility for your journey, this book is for you.

Contents

SECTION 1:

Preparation

Going through 10 breathwork sessions with a professional Rebirthing Breathworker is transformational journey and this journal will help you navigate through the sessions.

Correcting your breathing is just the beginning of the journey.

It is a journey of discovery, some things you may already know about and be able to go deeper into. Other things you discover may well surprise you.

This workbook gives you the pointers to probe into your inner journey.

Section 1: journalling before you start your breathwork journey.

Section 2:
After each session you are encouraged to reflect on what happened.

Section 3:
Gives you some theory and further topics which assist you on your journey of 10 sessions. These topics do not need to be completed in the order presented. Familiarise yourself

with each topic and then if the topic comes up in your session, it's a good time to do the work. You can discuss this with your Rebirther.

Don't get stuck in overthinking this process, let go of any need to do it right the first time! Because you can't get it wrong. Mind mastery is all about letting go of critical, unsupportive thoughts.

In case you run out of space to write, have another journalling book ready.

When you complete 10 sessions you may want to reflect more as more realisations are made.

Your First Few Breathwork Sessions

A session is usually done in a reclining position so that the body is relaxed. The purpose of each session is to guide the breathing rhythm until a completed energy cycle is achieved. The first five to twenty completed energy cycles, done perhaps one per week, seem to clear out enough physical tension and emotional blocks to enable people to practice conscious connected breathing alone.

Through connected breathing, unresolved emotional experiences, forgotten memories, buried feelings, energy blockages, belief systems and unconscious attitudes surface. So when experiencing connected breathing a person may feel sensations in their body both uncomfortable or enjoyable.

Connected breathing helps us move through any difficulties we may have experienced at birth and other traumatic events in our lifetime. As the breath and energy in the breath moves through the body any areas with emotional energetic blocks are released if you feel safe enough and are ready to release it.

When we feel safe enough we can also allow ourselves to feel suppressed feelings or emotions energetically to then let go of the stuckness. This may involve simply breathing through any uncomfortable sensations because it isn't necessary to re-experience the situation.

Your first session is longer because your Rebirther will need to ask you questions about your life history. Individual

Breathwork sessions can last between one and three hours. The initial sessions generally deal with resistances and defences we may have built up to protect ourselves.

These include:

- **Mind chatter**

Have you ever noticed how your thoughts race through your head? If you have ever practiced Mindfulness meditation you will understand that it is important to simply observe our thoughts and not to react to them. When we react to our thoughts we give them so much power. Just because we have a thought about something or someone, it doesn't mean that thought is actually real or true.

During a session all kinds of thoughts will come up for you. In particular, "Am I doing this right?" Your mind will distract you from doing circular breathing. You mind may try to confuse you by saying, "I don't get this, it's not working." This will cause you to get frustrated. It's important to recognise this and to not believe your thoughts, or react to them.

Of course, we do have useful thoughts and so it is important to discern between what is useful and what is exaggerated, dramatic or trying to run our lives.

The objective in a session is to maintain a connected breath and you can't do this if you are continually thinking.

- **Pausing between breaths**

When we are listening to our thoughts during a session we instinctively pause our breathing. Connected breathing involves connecting our inhalation to our exhalation and our exhalation to our inhalation. This is why it's important to keep the flow going and let go of your thoughts. When we stop connecting our breaths, we also stop the flow of energy.

Another reason for pausing between our breaths is resistance to feeling. In order to protect ourselves from uncomfortable feelings or emotions, by escaping. It may seem like you are drifting off and not in your body. Your Rebirther will notice this and keep you conscious.

• Disassociation

Anaesthesia derived from former medical procedures or birth (such as epidurals) can still be stored in the cells of the body. This also includes having used recreational drugs. Rebirthing can unlock these drugs for release. Whilst this is happening, you can feel drugged, spacey, relaxed and stop breathing for a moment. It is important for you to keep breathing because connected breathing clears the effect of anaesthesia from your body and you no longer fall asleep.

• Physically Tired

If you are physically tired when you start breathwork your body relaxes and this may cause you to drift off and want to sleep. Coming to a session in this state is a resistance to releasing your breathing mechanism or working through physical and emotional blocks. If you are hyperactive you tend to live on adrenaline. So when you start to do breathwork you also relax and want to sleep.

- **Tetany**

Which is a medical term when fingers becoming locked with painful cramping, this is an indication of holding on to deep fear. Sometimes this can last for a few sessions if it is deep. When energy is activated during connected breathing, the release of tension in the body can create vibrations. For some people, feeling the vibrations can freak them out. This causes tetany so it is important to trust that the energy vibrations are normal and even enjoy them! It is important to lengthen your breath and relax, this will always move you through tetany. You are encouraged to be loving towards yourself whilst taking soft and gentle breaths. You have allow yourself to feel safe and to let the energy do the work by letting go of the need to control it.

Connect your in-breath to your out-breath...

...and your out-breath to your in-breath.

Conscious connected breathing is also known as circular breathing and originally coined as rebirthing. This technique of breathing is helpful in alleviating anxiety, headaches, pain, worry, improves self esteem, it deepens meditation, expands awareness and so much more.

It was whilst taking a bath back in the 1970s that Leonard Orr the founder of this technique, started spontaneously regressing to a state of feeling like a helpless infant and he couldn't get out of the bath for 3 hours. He continued taking long baths and more prenatal and birth memories rose up.

He then experimented by using a snorkel to breathe with his head immersed under water. Whilst using the snorkel he discovered how circular breathing is crucial to moving through a difficult experience. He found that under water he was forced to keep breathing and breathed through any experiences which came up. With the help of friends they got together and helped each other get through their own experiences whilst breathing in a hot tub and thus, wet rebirthing was born. Leonard realised that the emotional pain of birth experiences for some people was just too overwhelming, even with what we consider as a normal birth in a hospital.

At the time, Frank Leboyer's book "Birth without violence" had been published and the long term impact of birth trauma on a person was beginning to be understood. Leonard realised it was better to start breathing sessions out of water, as this is more gentle and so dry rebirthing was born. During dry rebirthing sessions a person may uncover many other life incidents before they are ready to deal with birth.

Circular means that the inhalation merges with the exhalation and the exhalation merges with the inhalation. There was no pause in between breaths. This is the crucial component to breathing energy (prana or Chi) which moves around the body with the breath. Within the first few sessions the focus is initially on unblocking the breathing mechanism and releasing energy blocks which prevent the movement of energy through the body. This may be a discomfort in the body, a memory, a pain or a fear and no matter how difficult it may feel, the person is guided to breathe through the experience until they reach a state of relaxation. It is essential that you don't get trapped in the drama of it, by continuing to breathe an energetic or emotional release occurs.

Ciara's experience, "I trained with Leonard. When I first unblocked my breathing mechanism it felt like a pressure valve popped and I felt instant relief. The struggle to breathe was gone! It was wonderful to feel what is was like to breathe full breaths again which were long and gentle. Everyone has different life experiences and so, no two sessions are the same.

Your experience may be completely different to mine, so the blocks we have to breathing may be different. After I broke through this then the real work began – and I remember during sessions experiencing childhood situations, feel stuck and not wanting to move forward and be born. So much tension had been stored in my body. All kinds of feelings and sensations come up which can be difficult and I wanted to stop breathing but having the support of a Rebirther guiding you helps you move through the experience rather than giving up."

As children when a difficult experience came up we often suppressed it or were told we're not allowed to feel it.

Circular breathing allows that feeling to go through to completion without being suppressed. It's not easy and my mind played many tricks on me to try and make me stop, but I kept breathing through it and it was really worth it.

Memories were shown to me and I felt pain in my body, by continuing to breathe the pain gave way to coming to a place of peace and serenity. Sometimes my body felt like it was floating, I felt light and free – not a care in the world.

Most people need ten 1 to 2 hour sessions with a well trained Rebirther Breathworker in order to learn the skill of intuitive Breathing.

After we have learned it, we are able to maintain the connected breathing rhythm for at least an hour without supervision. We can then consciously breathe divine Energy every day or whenever we like.

Rebirthing is not only about the Breath

We take a wholistic approach - you embark on a journey to understand the whole of who you are. The ultimate aim is to Master your Life...

So we start with **Breath Mastery** and during your sessions you will initially experience resistance to free-flowing and expansive breathing. Having a high quality one one one session with a trained Rebirther is essential.

- It might be that you struggle to simply breathe in air continually, because the inhalation represents breathing life force energy into your body.
- It might be that you feel light headed because you're not used to breathing in so much
- It might be that you start feeling tingling or vibrations. These new sensations are wonderful however, some people may feel stressed because they've never felt anything like this before.
- It might be that you have suppressed some emotions and are resisting feeling them. It's important to trust that you simply breathe through whatever comes up for you and you do move through it.
- No matter what you experience in a session, you are supported and even if it feels difficult you breathe through it.
- Once you break through any resistances, then your breath flows which is enjoyable. Perhaps you'll make realisations about your life during this phase of the session. Perhaps you'll feel peace or bliss.

We also focus on **Mind Mastery** which means looking at your thoughts. Even during sessions you have to learn to quieten your stream of thoughts. Our mind wants to distract us from releasing and moving ahead in our lives. Our thinking is often the root of many of our life issues. Your Rebirther will coach you in how to review your thoughts. You soon learn how to become the master of your mind not the servant!

You will also be guided in spiritual purification practices with air, fire, water and earth to help you gain **Body Mastery**. This includes both our physical body and our energetic body.

When all of these techniques are combined you'll find that you increase your vitality and love of life.

Rebirthing isn't a one time experience

Every ten years (if not beforehand) it's beneficial to have sessions with an experienced rebirther. It is surprising how your breath can become inhibited if you're not working on your life circumstances. It took getting cancer for me to realise I needed to change being comfortable, be pushed again and work on an even deeper level.

Breathing Goals

Personal Development Goals

Preparing for a Breathwork Journey

Notice Your Breathing

As you go about your daily life notice how you breathe and make notes here:

What's your inhale like?

What's your exhale like?

Do you hold your breath?

Is your breathing difficult?

Do you have asthma/COPD/cystic fibrosis/allergies that impact breathing?

Do you breathe complete inhalations? Drawing in the air

Do you let your exhales all the way out?

How often do you pause your breath?

Does it feel good to breathe?

Are there jerks in the breath when you breathe?

Do you breathe in your abdomen or your chest?

Do you breathe in your whole body?

Where do you notice you breathe better? At home/out socially/workplace/school

Where do you notice your breathing is difficult? At home/out socially/workplace/school.

Do certain people cause you to hold your breath or to breathe easy? If so, who?

Notice if your breath seems different whilst standing, sitting, walking, or lying.

20 Connected Breaths

Before your session practice connecting your breaths. This is a simple exercise which you can do at any time to help calm and centre you: 20 connected breaths.

One cycle:
· Take a full breath in through the nose and connect the in-breath to the out breath
· Breathe out through the nose and connect the out-breath to the in-breath

Now do this cycle **four times** with four short but full breaths

And the final cycle is one long in-breath merging into a long out-breath.

· 4 cycles of shorter inhalations and exhalations
· 1 cycle of a longer inhalation and exhalation

Don't pause between the inhalation and the exhalation, or the exhalation and the inhalation.

My Life Story

Write the story of your life

Here are some points to consider:

Were you planned/wanted?
By both parents?
Did your mother/primary caregiver want a boy/girl
Did your father/primary caregiver want a boy/girl
How do you feel about your biological sex?
Which number child are you? Of how many children?
Are you an only child?
How did your other siblings react to your arrival?
Any illnesses, major accidents or injuries during or emotional traumas:
During infancy?
During childhood?
During teenage years?
Any deaths in your close family whilst growing up?
Were your parents divorced? Separated or deceased?
Describe your life as a child:
Describe your parent's/caregiver's relationship while you were growing up:
Were any significant others living with family? (grandparents, step-parents)
How was school? Did you like it? Were you bullied? Have any difficulty with teachers?
College/training/university/apprenticeship
What work do like/dislike?

How do you feel about being on your own? Alone?
Significant romantic relationships?
Relationship pros
Relationship cons
Any children?
Any major accidents/ailments/medical conditions when you were born, infancy, toddlerhood, childhood, teenage years, young adult, adult.

Current Personal Information

Do you like the way you look?
What do you like about your body?
What do you dislike about your body?
What are your major fears?
What in your life would you most like to change?
What would you like more of in your life?

SECTION 2:

Session 1

Date:

Breathworker:

Sex of Breathworker:

Did you arrive on time?
Notice if you had any resistance to doing the session. This
can happen on first and fourth sessions.

How were you before the session? Anything come up for you
in the few days beforehand?

How was your rapport with your Rebirther?

Did you have any physical discomfort during the session?
How comfortable were you lying down? Did you need extra
pillows for support? A blanket for warmth?

Was it a struggle to maintain the connected breath? Did you
try too hard?

Did you feel discomfort in your head/neck/chest from breathing?

What issues came up during your session?

Any realisations made?

Affirmations Given:

How was integration:

Reflections on the session:

The goal of the first few sessions is to actually notice how we are breathing and to learn how to maintain connecting our breaths gently, consciously and intuitively. In a way that activates our Divine Energy and cleans our energy body. This is what we call spiritual purification with air.

Session 2

Date:

Breathworker:

Sex of Breathworker:

Did you arrive on time?

How were you before the session? Anything come up for you in the few days beforehand?

How was your rapport with your Rebirther?

Did you have any physical discomfort during the session? How comfortable were you lying down? Did you need extra pillows for support? A blanket for warmth?

Was it a struggle to maintain the connected breath? Did you try too hard?

Did you feel discomfort in your head/neck/chest from breathing?

What issues came up during your session?

Any realisations made?

Affirmations Given:

How was integration:

Reflections on the session:

Session 3

Date:

Breathworker:

Sex of Breathworker:

Did you arrive on time?

How were you before the session? Anything come up for you in the few days beforehand?

How was your rapport with your Rebirther?

Did you have any physical discomfort during the session? How comfortable were you lying down? Did you need extra pillows for support? A blanket for warmth?

Was it a struggle to maintain the connected breath? Did you try too hard?

Did you feel discomfort in your head/neck/chest from breathing?

What issues came up during your session?

Any realisations made?

Affirmations Given:

How was integration:

Reflections on the session:

.

Session 4

Date:

Breathworker:

Sex of Breathworker:

Did you arrive on time?
Notice if you had any resistance to doing the session. This can happen on first and fourth sessions.

How were you before the session? Anything come up for you in the few days beforehand?

How are you getting along with your Rebirther? Take some time to consider if they remind you of any of your primary care-givers? Their mannerisms, voice, intonation, expressions. How do you react to this?

Did you have any physical discomfort during the session? How comfortable were you lying down? Did you need extra pillows for support? A blanket for warmth?

Was it a struggle to maintain the connected breath?

Did you experience any breathing deviations?

Did you release your breathing mechanism?

What issues came up during your session?

Any realisations made?

Affirmations Given:

How was integration:

Reflections on the session:

Session 5

Now that you are familiar with the reflection questions they are listed together with plenty of space to write in.

Reflections on the session:
Did you arrive on time?
How were you before the session? Anything come up for you in the few days beforehand?
How are you getting along with your Rebirther? Take some time to consider if they remind you of any of your primary care-givers? Their mannerisms, voice, intonation, expressions. How do you react to this?
Did you have any physical discomfort during the session?
How comfortable were you lying down? Did you need extra pillows for support? A blanket for warmth?
Was it a struggle to maintain the connected breath?
Did you experience any breathing deviations?
Did you release your breathing mechanism? Did any birth issues come up during your session?
What issues came up during your session?
Any realisations made?
Affirmations Given:
How was integration?

Session 6

Date:

Breathworker:

Sex of Breathworker:

Reflections on the session:
Did you arrive on time?
How were you before the session? Anything come up for you
in the few days beforehand?
How are you getting along with your Rebirther? Take some
time to consider if they remind you of any of your primary
care-givers? Their mannerisms, voice, intonation,
expressions. How do you react to this?
Did you have any physical discomfort during the session?
How comfortable were you lying down? Did you need extra
pillows for support? A blanket for warmth?
Was it a struggle to maintain the connected breath?
Did you experience any breathing deviations?
Did you release your breathing mechanism? Did any birth
issues come up during your session?
What issues came up during your session?
Any realisations made?
Affirmations Given:
How was integration:

Session 7

Date:

Breathworker:

Sex of Breathworker:

Reflections on the session:
Did you arrive on time?
How were you before the session? Anything come up for you in the few days beforehand?
How are you getting along with your Rebirther? Take some time to consider if they remind you of any of your primary care-givers? Their mannerisms, voice, intonation, expressions. How do you react to this?
Did you have any physical discomfort during the session?
How comfortable were you lying down? Did you need extra pillows for support? A blanket for warmth?
Was it a struggle to maintain the connected breath?
Did you experience any breathing deviations?
Did you release your breathing mechanism? Did any birth issues come up during your session?
What issues came up during your session?
Any realisations made?
Affirmations Given:
How was integration:

Session 8

Date:

Breathworker:

Sex of Breathworker:

Reflections on the session:
Did you arrive on time?
How were you before the session? Anything come up for you
in the few days beforehand?
How are you getting along with your Rebirther? Take some
time to consider if they remind you of any of your primary
care-givers? Their mannerisms, voice, intonation,
expressions. How do you react to this?
Did you have any physical discomfort during the session?
How comfortable were you lying down? Did you need extra
pillows for support? A blanket for warmth?
Was it a struggle to maintain the connected breath?
Did you experience any breathing deviations?
Did you release your breathing mechanism? Did any birth
issues come up during your session?
What issues came up during your session?
Any realisations made?
Affirmations Given:
How was integration:

Session 9

Date:

Breathworker:

Sex of Breathworker:

Reflections on the session:
Did you arrive on time?
How were you before the session? Anything come up for you
in the few days beforehand?
How are you getting along with your Rebirther? Take some
time to consider if they remind you of any of your primary
care-givers? Their mannerisms, voice, intonation,
expressions. How do you react to this?
Did you have any physical discomfort during the session?
How comfortable were you lying down? Did you need extra
pillows for support? A blanket for warmth?
Was it a struggle to maintain the connected breath?
Did you experience any breathing deviations?
Did you release your breathing mechanism? Did any birth
issues come up during your session?
What issues came up during your session?
Any realisations made?
Affirmations Given:
How was integration:

Session 10

Date:

Breathworker:

Sex of Breathworker:

Reflections on the session:
Did you arrive on time?
How were you before the session? Anything come up for you in the few days beforehand?
How are you getting along with your Rebirther? Take some time to consider if they remind you of any of your primary care-givers? Their mannerisms, voice, intonation, expressions. How do you react to this?
Did you have any physical discomfort during the session?
How comfortable were you lying down? Did you need extra pillows for support? A blanket for warmth?
Was it a struggle to maintain the connected breath?
Did you experience any breathing deviations?
Did you release your breathing mechanism? Did any birth issues come up during your session?
What issues came up during your session?
Any realisations made?
Affirmations Given:
How was integration:

Achieving these goals is a very valuable accomplishment and is a valuable investment in ourselves – in our health and well being on every level.

The Goals of the First Ten Rebirthing Breathwork Sessions

by Leonard Orr

1. Rebirthing or Conscious Connected Intuitive Breathing is learning to breathe energy (prana) as well as air. To have this ability available to us is the basic, most important goal of the first ten sessions. Ten 2 to 3-hour sessions is the responsible way to teach Rebirthing Breathwork.

2. Get past physiological drama.

3. Get past tetany (body cramping).

4. Get past psychological and emotional drama.

5. Experience the merging of the inner breath and the outer breath (breathing from the Breath Itself).

6. Relive the moment of the first breath and experience releasing the breathing mechanism.

7. Heal the headwaters of our Life spring – learn the healing power of conscious breathing.

8. Realize that the Breath is harmless and that the mind can be dangerous. Learn to process the mind with affirmations and emotional response techniques.

9. Learn Spiritual Purification.

10. Learn proper nutrition and the importance of vegetarianism.

11. Follow an exercise system and practice basic breathing exercises like 20 connected breaths and alternate nostril breathing, etc.

12. Develop the snorkel habit and learn the role of breathing in the bathtub.

13. Have an awareness of the 16 biggies of human trauma.

14. Be familiar with the spiritual purification practices: mind (mantra), earth, air, water and fire practices, and love.

15. Be aware of the spiritual costs of lifestyles and relationships.

16. Learn to manage emotional energy pollution (EEP) from others, especially in public places.

17. Be able to breathe for an hour without supervision.

18. Become aware of our Natural Divinity.

19. Become aware of spiritual, mental and physical enlightenment.

20. Realize that spiritual enlightenment can occur in a five minute span of time, whereas mental enlightenment takes 50 – 100 years and physical enlightenment takes 500 or more years.

21. Raise Kundalini energy, the Holy Spirit, breathing Divine Energy.

22. Become familiar with the Physical Immortality philosophy and affirmations, and the Owner's Manual (by Leonard Orr)

23. Become familiar with the basics of childbirth education.

24. Realize the role of money and prosperity consciousness in our relationship with Breathwork professionals.

25. Realize that healing yourself always comes first.

26. Learn to heal the death urge.

Leonard has many of his personal rebirthing clients go through what we might call the ideal rebirthing sequence.

The **first** dry session is a powerful cycle which usually contains paralysis that people go through rather efficiently because they are willing to follow instructions.

The **second** session is 4 to 10 days later, after person has had time to rest and integrate the first one. It is the heaviest and longest until the rebirthee is willing to let go completely and feel safe enough to permit the energy to overwhelm them and do its healing work.

The **third** session is what Leonard Orr called the scary one, because the rebirth seems to be going smoothly and all once the throat constricts all the internal fluids are generated that caused the rebirth and to choke and strangle. There is fear of death from clogged air passages and inability to breathe. When the Rebirther reminds the Rebirthee that it is a Memory and encourages them to relax, then the panic subsides and it's breathed out in several cycles. The third session is more intense, but usually shorter than number two.

The **fourth** session is what you might call a re-run of parts of all three, but also has unique characteristics of its own.

Throughout the **fifth** session, which can also be described as a re-run, the Rebirther is able to breathe smoothly and rhythmically without fear. It usually takes half as long as number two, for example. This brings about Rebirthings, which are pleasurable and interesting, make realisations.

Don't take this prices for granted too soon and too easily. Just because you've done 10 sessions doesn't mean you're done. Going for the drama and "acting out" instead of going for the release through breathing can make this level of clarity take dozens or hundreds of sessions to get to the same point.

Even leaders in the field of Breathwork need occasional ongoing support and have facilitated sessions, working on their life circumstances. It's important not to think you're above doing this work whatever stage you're at. It's important to have 10 facilitated sessions every decade or even less than that.

SECTION 3:

1. Session Experiences

These are some experiences that can happen during the first few sessions. Your Rebirther knows how to guide you if any of them happen to you.

This is a list of many things that *can* happen during a session.

It is vital to note that we are all different, so some things may happen to you and other things may not.

DO NOT USE THIS AS A CHECKLIST OF THINGS YOU *HAVE TO* EXPERIENCE

Comfort
· How comfortable were you?
· Any lower back discomfort? Shoulders?
· Did your body temperature change during the session?
· Your body temperature feels hot and sometimes you may sweat.
· Your body temperature gets much cooler and the person needs a blanket.

Breathing
· Did you stop connecting your breaths?

- Did you feel anxious about not being able to do the breathing properly?
- Did you push yourself hard to breathe the connected breath?
- Did you control your inhalation and exhalation?
- Did you feeling like it was hard to breathe.

Thinking
- Did you find that you stopped thinking as much
- Were you able to quieten your thoughts?
- Did you break through self-criticism?
- Did any fear that you are not in control come up – panic, anxiety?

Physical sensations
- Did your jaw feel tight and it felt difficult to speak.
- Did you jaw clench and you couldn't speak.
- As the energy starts moving did you get tingling feelings in any of these areas: hands, arms, feet, legs.
- Did you feel pins and needles?
- Did your arms or feet feel like they were blocks of wood and feel numb or even paralysis?
- Did the muscles of your hands or feet feel like they were frozen into claws and begin throbbing with pain.
- Did you have any cramping, tetany or body pains?
- Tingling starts again and the out-breath relaxes.
- Did your chest feel really tight and lungs feel constricted, and then found it hard to breathe?
- What other body sensations did you feel?
- Tense forehead/shoulders/arms/abdomen/legs.

- Any feelings of paralysis ?
- You may smell the odour of anaesthetic, choloform or any other drugs used during the birth process or even infant experiences.
- Did you have a metallic taste in your mouth/nose/throat?
- Did you have any light floating feelings in head or all of body?
- Did you bring up any phelgm or spit?

Emotions
- Did you fall asleep or go unconscious during the session?
- Did any difficult emotions come up for you? Sadness, grief, anger, bitterness, hate
- Did you stop yourself from feeling any emotions?
- Did you feel hungry during your session?
- Did you not feel anything during your session?
- Did you have any memories?
- Were you scared or felt fear?
- Did you get any images from your life?
- Did you feel any releases during your session?

Trust
- Feeling Safe
- Establishing Trust
- Did you notice getting irritated/annoyed/uncomfortable with your Breathworker?
- Does your Breathworker remind you of anyone?

Flow and peace
- Did you surrender to resisting and relax?

- Did you reach a point where your breathing flowed?
- What energy sensations did you feel in your body?
- Did you feel any waves of intense pleasure?
- Did you feel/visualise any waves of intense light coming into your body/surrounding you?
- What are the sensations/what does it feel like when you connect to Divine energy?
- Did you have any visions/hear guidance/mystical experiences?

As you progress through your sessions come back to this list and notice what else you may have experienced.

2. Breath Mastery

Breath mastery produces an experience of the body as an energy system that can be healthy and calm, in which a blissful state of mind becomes the norm. After ten to twenty sessions, the accumulated tension of a lifetime gets dissolved and daily practice maintains a wonderful state of spiritual purification with the air element. A relaxed, intuitive breathing rhythm is the key.

Breathing Deviations
Breathing deviations are unconscious defence mechanisms which you subconsciously put in place to avoid feeling and remembering.

You naturally breathed fully and freely when you were a baby. As you grew up circumstances would happen or you felt sensations which you perceived as uncomfortable, difficult or scary. So you unconsciously blocked parts of your breathing mechanism by freezing, controlling or holding your breath so that you would not feel what was happening.

These breathing responses created breathing deviations, which inhibited your natural breath. Different breathing deviations can be associated with different life circumstances, responses and thoughts. Releasing a breathing deviation helps to let go of a belief or story and allows more energy to move through your body.

During your sessions you'll notice your Rebirther guiding you, for instance they might say, "relax your inhalation."

Mind mastery is an aspect of releasing a breathing deviation, when you release the underlying it helps change the perception of events associated with the breathing deviation, as well as your attitude towards life.

If you have done many group sessions and/or mouth breathing sessions, it might take a while until you can move through breathing deviations and open your breathing mechanism.

This is because sometimes practising inappropriate ways of breathing can actually strengthen breathing deviations and maintain defence mechanisms.

Poor breathing styles include;
· forcing the inhale
· pushing the exhale
· breathing too lightly
· breathing too strongly
· breathing too slowly
· breathing too quickly
· controlling your breath
· pausing before the inhalation
· pausing before the exhalation
· inhalation and exhalation are mechanical - there's no joy in the inhalation and no letting go in the exhalation

- continually making loud noises whilst breathing
- the inhalation is shorter than the exhalation
- the exhalation is shorter than the inhalation
- not observing and being in contact with emotions,
- having specific expectations with the sessions,
- being addicted to intense sensations, and
- not surrendering to the process

Liberating these breathing deviations through Rebirthing opens you up to fully embracing life, allowing life force energy to move through you without restrictions, allowing you to re-experience child-like joy and freedom.

3. Letting Go of Drama

With most people emotional and physical drama stops within ten sessions, and they are able to maintain a connected breathing rhythm without drama for one hour.

With regular practice of the breathing rhythm over a long period, rebirthing produces less and less eventful sessions.

Physical Drama
Tetany
Disassociation
Shaking
Tensions
Pins and needles
Paralysis
Feeling hot and cold
Sweating
Dizziness
Heaviness in the chest
Blocked nose

Emotional Drama
It is important to feel emotions but the key is to allow them and move through the experience by trusting the process. Emoting is encouraged and emotional releases are incredibly important. Some people think that if they cry, because they

have held on to it for so long, they will never stop. Your Rebirther will guide you through.

Whatever comes up for you, you'll be guided to feel it and then experience what it's like to move on. Allow the breath to safely guide you through the sensations. This is because prolonged screaming, bawling, anger or needing intensity to feel like you've had a good session can become a habit.

Releasing is necessary but getting stuck isn't the objective. Everyone works at a different pace so this could happen in one session or over a course of sessions.

After ten sessions or as soon a dramatic psychological or emotional drama stops, which may be before or after ten sessions, you should start rebirthing yourself. You should continue rebirthing yourself until you can maintain a relaxed connected intuitive breathing rhythm for at least an hour. At this point, you should practice doing twenty connected breaths whenever you feel like it, especially when you are uptight or angry or experiencing other physical or emotional drama.

This is one of the basic goals of our first ten sessions to get past the physiological sensations and emotional drama. Breathwork is not about drama or therapy – it is about learning conscious energy breathing. Breathwork is a very specific skill that everybody can and should learn. It may be the supreme tool for relaxing the mind and body. When we get passed the physiological and emotional drama during our first few sessions we then experience gently, very pleasurable Divine energy flows. It is difficult to have relaxation and dis-ease in the same space at the same time. Relaxation cancels fear and dis-ease.

Notice in your life your addictions to drama, you may not even realise you're doing it.

Are you dramatic?
Do you overreact?
Do you thrive/feel alive when things get dramatic?

Attracting dramatic people in your life can often be as a result of this happening in your family.

For instance, if your father gets angry and has outbursts this can become an unconscious desire to attract angry people into your life. This is how love is shown to you, consider that anger could mean love to you.

How does drama come up in your life?

4. The Personal Law Process

You will do this process with your Rebirther. If you haven't, then the seminar process is available on [Amazon](#) Personal Law Process: The Biggest Lie You Create About Yourself.

List 3 things you like about yourself

_____

_____

_____

List 3 things you dislike about yourself

_____

_____

_____

List 3 things you liked about your mother/primary carer:

_____

_____

_____

List 3 things you disliked about your mother/primary carer:

List 3 things you liked about your father/primary carer

List 3 things you disliked about your father/primary carer:

List 3 things you like about your sibling

List 3 things you disliked about your sibling

List 3 things you like about your sibling

List 3 things you disliked about your sibling

My Personal Law:

My Eternal Law:

My Specific Negatives:

My Mantras for the Specific Negatives:

Reflection on how my Personal Law acts out in my life:

5. The Energy Cycle

During a breathwork session you'll notice that different stages arise as you go through the cycle. The early stage may repeat before you surrender and enter a flowing breath.

Sharing: before connected breathing begins

- Start connected breathing
- Energy starts flowing
- Resistance
- Breathing deviations

Ascending Phase
This may happen once or repeat a few times

- Energy peak and energy release

Peak Phase
This leads to either repeating the ascending phase again or moving on to the descending phase

The above steps might repeat a few times or lead to the descending phase.

- Breath flows
- Surrender letting go and relaxation
- Completion

Descending Phase
Peace/bliss

Integration: back to normal breathing

The Energy Release

At some time in Rebirthing there is a reconnection to Divine Energy and as a result you may experience tingling and vibrating in your body.

It can happen in any location in your body and sometimes felt throughout the whole body.

When the energy/prana you breath in meets tension in your body, your body responds by tingling and vibrating.

Allow yourself to feel this and if you can, enjoy it.

If you get freaked out by it because you can't control it, you may end up with tetany.

Resistance to the flowing of energy can also cause tetany.

The tingling and vibrations clears fear and resistance so it should be encouraged.

If you don't experience tingling and vibrations - that's ok.

At the energy peak resistance is dissolved and you breathe faster and there is no tingling.

Breathing faster after the energy peak is ok, it's not hyperventilation, you feel an increase in vitality.

Your mind has surrendered to the experience and you move into peace/bliss. Your mind and body are in harmony with each other.

During the descending phase you feel renewed and this is also why the technique is called Rebirthing, because in each session the divine infant is reborn in human flesh.

The energy release is actually dissolving resistance to Divine Energy.

What has your experience of the energy cycle been?

Chest and Abdomen Releases

In you first few sessions you may have chest or abdomen breathing releases. Breathing fully in these areas gets blocked as a result of difficult life experiences. Tension, stress, fear can be stored in your chest or abdomen which causes you to struggle to maintain a connected breath during a session. The struggle to inhale may cause you to move your head/shoulders upwards in a forward motion as you inhale. Tension and tightness in the abdomen or chest can be a result of breathing deviations or your struggle to breathe your first breath.

The Breathing Release

The breathing release, is about reliving the moment of our first breath at birth and releasing the fear and trauma that has been restricting our breathing ability ever since. A breathing release brings about a permanent and effortless transformation of our breathing mechanism. Releasing this birth trauma memory may or may not occur during the first ten sessions. It could take years. When it does happen, it has a powerful impact on our ability to breathe fully and embrace life. It is a release of all your resistance to life.

The breathing release happens when you feel safe enough to re-live the moment of your first breath. It is physiologically, psychologically, and spiritually reliving the moment when you started breathing for the first time.

The breathing mechanism is freed and transforms so that, from then on, you know when your breathing is inhibited and you can correct it. Don't think that once your breathing mechanism has released that you're done. Life's stresses continue and this causes our breathing mechanism to get restricted.

The breathing mechanism may release incrementally in all palpable rebirth experiences. This is because you need to feel safe enough to go through it and so it releases little by little until you're ready.

This all depends on what your first breath was actually like. Your Rebirther recognises all of the reactions you can have so they can safely guide you through. When you are more comfortable with the vibrating energy, and when it goes through the throat area, you may feel constricted and feel like you're choking. For some people this is what happened when they took their first breath because the umbilical cord was cut before they learned to breathe, and they were choking on amniotic fluid and couldn't breathe.

The harder it was for you to take your first breath, the more you need to be ready to re-experiencing it and moving through it.

If you had a cord around your neck it would have been more of a struggle. If the epidural drugs were in your system you wouldn't be able to feel and might have been groggy. There are so many factors which impact your ability to take your first breath. So it's really important not to have any expectations about it.

Moving from a protected, warm environment in which your needs were met, out into a cold room is traumatic itself. Then, bam you have to take your first breath!

Understand that not everyone goes through this. For some people their first breath came easily.

6. Conception & Birth

Your Conception & Birth

Find out as much as you can about your conception & birth. If it's not possible to ask your parents or are there any other relatives who may know? Please don't get stressed about getting this information, because sometimes even mothers forget.

Were you planned? An accident?

Conceived naturally or artificial insemination?

Was alcohol or drugs taken?

Any miscarriages/foetal deaths/terminations before your birth?

If so, how do you feel about this?

Did your parents/primary care-givers live together during your pre-natal life?

What was the financial status of your family during your prenatal life?

What did your parents/primary care-givers tell you about your prenatal life?

Any complications during your mother's pregnancy?

Date and time of birth:

Place of birth? Hospital, home, car?

Was there an obstetrician present? Male or female?

Was anyone else present at your birth?

Was your labour: easy, long, difficult, short?

Other comments about your labour

Where was your father during your birth?

Do any of the following apply to your birth?
Twin
Premature
Overdue
Forceps delivery
Anaesthetised
Vaginal/Caesarean
Breach
Blue baby
Dry birth
Cord around your neck
Separated from your mother
Were you injured? Dislocated shoulder, cut by a scalpel
RH factor
Deformity
Placenta previa
Jaundice
Transfusion
Circumcision
Is there anything else about your birth you'd like to add:

Did your mother have any of these complications?
Haemorrhage
Infection
Episiotomy
Postpartum depression

Where are you breastfed? How long for? If not, why?

Do you have children?

Review the previous section and journal about your experiences.

Conceiving your child/children

Difficulties in conceiving or not able to conceive

Pregnancy

Miscarriages

Terminations

Giving birth (mother) or witnessing birth (father) It is important to work on releasing any guilt/regrets you may be holding on to.

7. Family Dynamics

A common occurrence in psychotherapy is transference, in which the client projects aspects of their primary care-giver on to the therapist. Generally, father issues are projected on to a male therapist and mother issues onto a female therapist. But this may not have been the case for you. You may have only had one care-giver, two care-givers of the same sex, grandparents caring for you or foster/adoptive parents.

So the qualities of your care-giver/s will be projected on to your Rebirther. Or if a care-giver wasn't present then you may project, "you're not here for me," on to your Rebirther.

Difficult reactions you may have towards your Rebirther may be reminding you of a care-giver. Take some time to consider whether you are projecting any traits of your care-giver/s on to your Rebirther.

Also consider your relationship with authority figures such as teachers.

Sibling relationships or if you didn't have siblings, how was that for you?

What was your relationship or lack of relationship with your grandparents like for you?

8. Purification With the Elements

As you go through your journey of 10 sessions it is recommended to also try purification with the elements. These practices are also great when it all gets a bit much, you feel drained or you simply want to become clearer.

Purification with the elements means that our emotional energy body is cleaned through basic practices with earth, air, water and fire.

By doing these practices your life energy is renewed. Simply sitting with candles or by a fire can renew you and increase your vitality and creativity. It is without a doubt, that we physically feel better when the energy body is clean and balanced.

Leonard Orr the founder of Rebirthing Breathwork spent many years reading the Vedic texts and learnt these techniques by observing yogis. These purification techniques will help you and you'll feel the difference:

The basic **Air** spiritual purification practice is what you're already doing conscious energy breathing. If you know pranayama exercises these also help clean the energy body.

The basic **Earth** spiritual purification practices are fasting, proper healthy diet (preferably vegetarian) and exercise. If you haven't fasted before take it slowly;
- first cut out meat and carbohydrates for a day,
- then only eat two meals between the hours of 10am and 4pm,
- progress to only drinking fresh juices for a day, and
- when you master that try water fasting.

Liquid fasting for three days helps to renew your digestive system.

Progress through these stages slowly. It is really important to be sensible and responsible for yourself.   If you have difficulties, stop fasting.

Earth purification also involves movement: exercise, singing, dancing, drumming, walking in nature, earthing - walk barefoot in your garden or lie down on the grass.

Experiences with Earth purification:

The basic **Water** spiritual purification practices are bathing twice per day and drinking clean water to make sure you are well hydrated. Yogis tend to bathe in rivers before sunrise and before sunset clearing their energy system with clean flowing water. Water helps clean our emotions so don't share water used for purification.

It is best to take a warm water bath or go in the hot tub. It's a good idea to buy a waterproof pillow to rest your head on when you're not submerging fully in it. Change the water if you use a hot tub. If you go to a hot springs make sure there is a flow of water. Bathing in water is not only a great purification technique, it's also a treat to float in the water and allow your mind to still.

Children's inflatable paddling pools work as a great alternative and can be bought cheaply. Fill it in your shower or wet room.

Experiences with Water:

The basic **Fire** spiritual purification practice is sitting with an open flame. If you have an indoor fire stove this is perfect.

Fire safety is of utmost importance when using fire purification, be responsible when using fire. When you're outside you need to physically contain the fire by using a fire pit, this can be a metal structure or a ring of stones.

As an alternative, you can easily buy a metal tray with tall sides and place candles in the tray. For tall candles make sure that if they fall over, they won't fall outside the metal tray - so nothing is burnt.

It is recommended to sit with the fire for a minimum of one hour, allowing the mental dross to be burnt away. Sitting with the fire stimulates and opens our chakras and cleanses them. For this reason it is important to do fire purification on your own and without speaking to other people.

Keep taking some nice deep breaths as you sit with the fire. Fire helps our mind calm, so if your mind chatter is going wild, take some time out, sit with fire and just let go! It is important to observe your thoughts as you would in mindfulness meditations. Don't attach to your thoughts, simply observe them and let them go.

Remember when you were a child and you would lie on the ground looking up at the clouds passing by? When using the mindfulness technique you are asked to observe your inhalation and exhalation. Then when you have a thought, view it as if it was a cloud passing by in the sky. Let your thoughts simply pass by. Do not identify with them. This is what is meant by non-attachment and assists us with our next spiritual.

Experiences with Fire:

You may be drawn to one element to find out what its effect is like, but also try those that you might be resistant to! Sometimes you may find resistance to using the element that will help you the most, so push through your resistance and try it. Trust in the process because spiritual purification really does become pleasurable!

Resistances to doing purification:

9. Forgiveness

Forgiveness is about letting go of hurts, resentments and negative thoughts about a person.

Writing completion letters to your mother, father, primary care-giver/s (the person/people who primarily looked after you as a child) are a great exercise in acknowledging and releasing destructive emotions, hurts and resentments.

Being honest with yourself is vital to this process. It is important not to ignore the difficult things that happened to you, however small they may seem to you, or your thoughts and feelings.

When you have completed these letters, talk about them with your rebirther.

First Letter:
Write all the limitations and destructive features of your relationship with each of your parents/care-givers. In this letter you can vent off and take no responsibility for anything you say. Express all your feelings you have about the way that you were treated by your parents/care-givers. It's okay to express anger, hatred and even insults. Once you have written this letter to each person you can now let it go and burn it.

First primary care-giver

Second primary care-giver/including if they weren't present or if you didn't know them.

Second Letter:

The second letter is a letter of thanks in which you express all the good things about your parents. In every relationship there is always something positive. Think about the wonderful things they did for you. It's important to thank them for bringing you into this life.

First primary care-giver

Second care-giver/including if they weren't present or you didn't know them.

Third Letter:

Now that you have expressed unprocessed emotions and you have more clarity regarding the relationship. This letter involves taking responsibility for the co-creation of this relationship and becoming objective.

First of all make an objective summary of what has happened and what is happening and what emotions are in play.

In the second part make a series of decisions about changing your own attitude and in some and how to make this relationship better.

What healthy suggestions can you make to improve this relationship?

The important Thing is to be able to express what we want positively and to know how to lovingly set boundaries.

First primary care-giver

Continued: and/or what boundaries do I need to learn with this person?

Second primary care-giver/including if they weren't present or you didn't know them.

Continued: and/or what boundaries do I need to learn with this person?

Your mental wellbeing, physical safety are paramount. Always remain safe, you don't need to continue a relationship with a person you don't feel safe with.

Give yourself time to work on your boundaries of what you will accept and what you won't.

Because you make a shift, it's really important to understand that the other person probably hasn't.

If the person is still alive don't expect them to behave differently, this is about you dealing with your feelings.

If they have not met your basic needs, don't expect them to, you can't change them.

Forgiveness helps us get closure in relationships, if that person wasn't present in our lives.

10. Your Journey Continues

Now you have completed 10 sessions create space in your life for your breathwork journey to continue.

- Consider doing a group retreat or training and you'll experience the dynamics that come to play with other participants.
- Experience purification with the elements at a retreat.
- Try warm water rebirthing with a facilitator.
- Try other personal/spiritual development techniques.

The next pages are for you to continue your inner journey and find the inspiration to create the life you want.

Made in the USA
Las Vegas, NV
05 May 2023

71558924R00083